# BILLION DOLLAR MIND

---

Practical Guide for Mental Strength
in the Game of Life

---

Rick Macci and
Nivedita (Niva) Uberoi Jerath MD, MS

BILLION DOLLAR MIND

Copyright © 2023 by

Nivedita (Niva) Uberoi Jerath MD, MS and Rick Macci

# DEDICATION

Rick Macci: This book is dedicated to the world. Even though I have been fortunate to be on a tennis court my whole life, I have not just changed strokes, but have also changed lives. In fact, I'm more of a life coach than a tennis coach. Everyone needs a mentor, everyone needs a pat on the back, and everyone needs motivation. I've been wired with those unreal Midwest values growing up in Greenville, Ohio and treating others even better than I treat myself. With this book, I want to share it with the world, because I really feel that's always been my calling and if the reader can even change **ONE** mindset, we all have won **WON.**

Dr. Nivedita (Niva) Jerath: This book is dedicated to my parents and to my two beautiful incredibly intelligent daughters, Athma and Ziva. To my mom, Veena Uberoi Jerath, who taught me about mental strength at a young age. While she corrected my tennis technique at age 11, I felt she needed only to praise me. Mom responded by telling me I needed "to develop a strong mind to handle criticism, feedback, and pressure to achieve great heights in life." Since that day, I became passionate about developing a strong mind, which helped me achieve in all the areas of my life, not just in tennis. To my dad, Mohan Jerath, who kept books written by

Normal Vincent Peale around our house. To this day, I remember that when I was 7, he told me the one thing we can always control regardless of the situation is our attitude. He would say, "It's our attitude, not our aptitude that determines our altitude." To my daughters, Athma and Ziva, and all the children of the world: I hope you use this book to build such a strong mind that nothing can disturb or bother you and you can succeed no matter what happens around you.

# TABLE OF CONTENTS

# INTRODUCTION

**"The difference in building a world class champion from the ground floor compared to building a world class building starting on the ground floor is by a few inches from one ear to another. Mental strength is stronger than physical strength."**

*-Rick Macci*

The human mind is the key to success and failure in life. Conquering one's mind is equivalent to conquering the world. This book is intended to help you build a "billion dollar mind" with the help of our practical techniques.

The human mind is immensely powerful but complex as a result of 100 billion neurons and 100 trillion connections in the brain. Because of the complexity, it is important to program our mind to our advantage. We have to train our mind, feed our mind, and build our mind so we can succeed. The evolutionary aspects of our mind resort to fear, anxiety, negativity, or excessive thoughts that flip flop and are not real. This purpose of this book is to help us become aware of our mental weaknesses and make changes in our thought process so we can use our mind to our advantage.

A good analogy of a strong human mind is comparing it to the human body. We frequently focus on providing our body with a healthy diet and exercise regimen to enhance our physical capabilities. In the same light, let's provide our mind with a healthy diet of positive sensory inputs to maximize its performance.

The mind is an extension of the brain and nervous system so we begin with a brief overview of neuroanatomy.

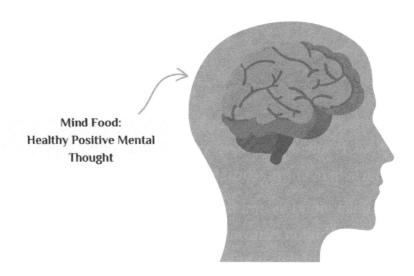

**Mind Food:**
**Healthy Positive Mental**
**Thought**

**Disclaimer:** This book is not for everyone. It is intended for those wanting to create a higher level of success, happiness, and fulfillment in life. It is designed as a focused book, which is advantageous, because there are fundamentals that require mastery, repetition, and most probably a re-read.

# ONE

# ACTION AS AN EXTENSION OF THE NERVOUS SYSTEM

**"The mind controls the body
and you control the mind."**
*- Rick Macci*

The nervous system is mainly divided into two main sections: the central nervous system, which comprises the brain and spinal cord, and the peripheral nervous system, which comprises nerves. The nerves are divided into two major categories called motor and sensory. The motor nerves help carry out an action, and the sensory nerves help relay sensory information to the body.

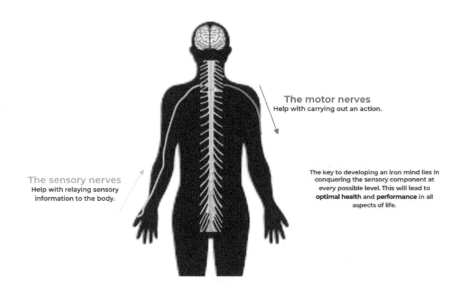

The motor nerves
Help with carrying out an action.

The sensory nerves
Help with relaying sensory
information to the body.

The key to developing an iron mind lies in
conquering the sensory component at
every possible level. This will lead to
**optimal health** and **performance** in all
aspects of life.

Simply put, the primary input is sensory, and the main output is motor. Sensory input involves a variety of sensations in the body; the motor output involves muscle movement and action. The sensory system is an important system that involves multiple sensations we learn in grade school: taste, touch, smell, sound, vision, and hearing. For the body, it detects touch, including pressure, pain, temperature, and body position.

**A critical point to remember is that controlling the sensory input helps control the motor output or action and is the key to developing a billion-dollar mind.**

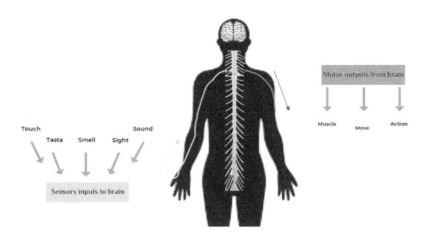

To add one more layer of complexity, we are going to go from sensory to motor, and between these two is the mind. Although the mind is immediately processed through our basic senses, the senses get stored in complex memories and form matrices, or thought processes and responses, that affect our actions. The mind is complex and composed of sensory input, which triggers thoughts, memories, and emotions (our limbic system).

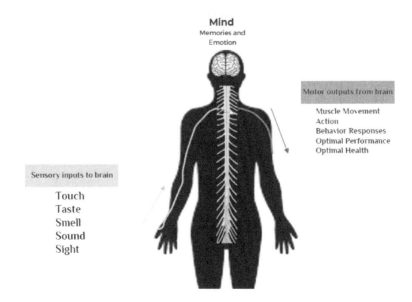

If our minds work optimally with the correct sensory input, maximizing every aspect of this input, although minor in the short run, can make a major long-term effect in mental strength.

Focusing on the senses would include the sense of smell, for instance. If associated with a positive memory or thought, this sense can generate positivity and confidence. Taste also can be optimized with certain foods, generating a positive mindset. Touch can be optimized with the feel of specific clothing, soft items, or even a kitten or dog that could help generate positive thoughts and ultimately a happy sensation resulting in a positive outcome. Listening to a particular song can also produce a confident, positive mindset. This can be seen frequently in practices or pep rallies that allow the mind to be focused and positive with the appropriate sensory input. Sight is also crucial; seeing externally something pleasant and visualizing internally can result in a positive outcome.

Although this could be considered a practical version of mindfulness, but instead of simply enjoying and focusing on the sensations of the present moment, this chapter, and this book, focuses on a personalized solution to help you maximize confidence and happiness. Our bodies prefer certain senses that produce positive emotions, and we need to be aware of these sensations.

"It can be the little things in life—soft touch, a smile, our own thoughts, and lovely flowers that can provide comfort and are important to our mental health."

Dr. Niva

**Practical Exercise:** Spend time with yourself and write down the taste of food that made you the happiest, your favorite song that put you in a good mood, your favorite smell or perfume, the touch that you want to feel again, and the visualization that puts a smile on your face. Optimize these sensations every day to create the best version of you.

_____

_____

_____

_____

_____

_____

_____

_____

_____

_____

_____

_____

_____

_____

# TWO

# BASIC CONTROL OF THE SENSORY INPUT

**"You control the situation. Do not
let the situation control you."**
*--Rick Macci*

Our sensations are many and infiltrate into memory and emotion, producing specific actions. If we can control our sensory input, we can better control our mind and actions. As described in this guide, remember it's a personal journey. Not everyone responds to sensory input in the same way.

For example, when Rick Macci was playing in a tennis tournament, he didn't notice a large parade outside the match despite that his opponent was banging his racket, upset and frustrated with the external sensory environment. While reading this book, remember you're taking a personal journey through your mind by:

#1 Recognizing your true passion in your life; thinking of things that you do when no one is watching. Why do you do them?

#2 Recognizing mental loops that are not in your favor. What can be done with the time we spend alone with our thoughts or during meditation?

#3 Immediately recognizing sensory input that is defeating; this is different for everyone. Handling challenging sensory input is discussed later on in the text.

#4 Producing personal sensory input that is high-performing and healthy. Be your own advocate. You want mental toughness and focus to help you reach your goals. This might include certain routines that help focus your mind before an event, competition, or performance.

## Thinking Loops

Thinking patterns can form a thinking loop, which are automatic thought processes that are generated over time. It is important to analyze each thought generated and objectively ask yourself if that thought is valid, helpful, or necessary. Analyzing one's thoughts is a crucial component of a billion dollar mind; however navigating thinking loops is deeply personal as thoughts can be a complicated web of patterns from the past and can have the potential to hinder a desired outcome.

Thinking loops are important because our minds are like a computer. A recurrent thought or thought process that doesn't help you, is similar to a virus in your brain and can affect your mental power, efficiency, and productivity.

A thinking loop can be generated from an external sensory stimuli or an internal thought that triggers a cascade of other thoughts, which can then result in a certain motor performance.

If for instance, the internal thought generated is one of anxiety or fear, this can trigger a feeling of tightness in the body. If, however, the thought generated is one of happiness and joy, this thought can generate relaxation in the body. The thinking loop below demonstrates how certain sensory inputs, if negative, can affect motor performance and can potentially create a suboptimal outcome.

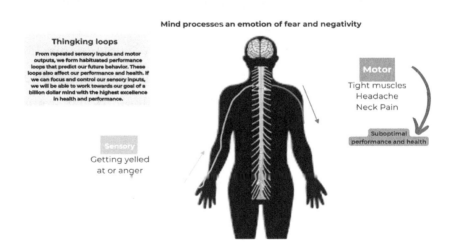

Mind processes an emotion of fear and negativity

**Thingking loops**

From repeated sensory inputs and motor outputs, we form habituated performance loops that predict our future behavior. These loops also affect our performance and health. If we can focus and control our sensory inputs, we will be able to work towards our goal of a billion dollar mind with the highest excellence in health and performance.

Motor
Tight muscles
Headache
Neck Pain

Suboptimal performance and health

Sensory
Getting yelled at or anger

**Practical Exercise**

Find your passions, preferences, and sensory stimuli that enhance or distract you from performance; identify recurrent thought-loops with each behavior. Write these down in a journal using the following processes.

Make it an active practice to watch repeated behavior patterns coupled with specific thinking processes.

_____

_____

_____

_____

_____

List sensory triggers that can either help or hinder your performance.

_____

_____

_____

_____

_____

Commit to continuing behaviors that optimize and enhance your success.

_____

_____

_____

_____

_____

_____

_____

_____

_____

_____

_____

_____

_____

_____

_____

_____

_____

# THREE

# IMPROVE SENSORY INPUT THROUGH POSITIVE AFFIRMATIONS

**"Every day, say to yourself powerful positive, motivating words, and you will be amazed it is better than any energy drink on the market."**

*- Rick Macci*

Is it such an irony that our brains are hardwired to think negatively, yet positivity is the mainstay for success. Whenever we take a picture or do something with others, our minds immediately jump to the one thing that went wrong or looked wrong rather than the thousands of things that went right. We are hardwired to think negatively. Negative thoughts are like deadweights destined for failure. In the same instance, a negative thought can turn positive, and our entire mood, attitude, energy, and productivity can change. With positive affirmations, your mind can maintain a more positive baseline state.

Dr. Niva Jerath's personal story: As a child, the only reason why Niva was undefeated in tennis for years in the Southern region of the United States was that she would spend at least half an hour upon waking with positive statements and positive affirmations—so much so that she convinced herself of her guaranteed win before she'd even stepped onto the court.

## Positivity = Winning

Negativity only hurts your true self and causes your inner voice to get upset, destabilizing your peace. Negativity is a surefire way to fail.

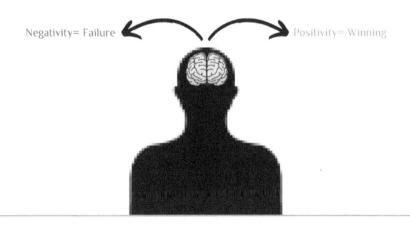

Negativity= Failure ← → Positivity= Winning

"One positive thought can make all the difference." Dr. Niva

**Practical Exercise**

Say 10 positive affirmations every day. Put these affirmations on your phone, computer, sport bags, or anywhere you routinely check. Use these examples and create your own:

- I love myself even if I make a mistake or lose a match or don't achieve my goal.
- I am not the outcome; I am a beautiful soul.
- I believe in myself.
- I am a winner.
- I am comfortable being Number 1.
- Nature creates beautiful things; I am a part of nature and am beautiful in every way.
- I actively practice saying positive things to myself.
- I give 100% every day.
- I do just a little extra to move from ordinary to extraordinary.

_____

_____

_____

_____

_____

_____

_____

# FOUR

# IMPROVE SENSORY INPUT THROUGH POSITIVE ASSOCIATIONS

**"The best gas to fill up your tank is not at the fuel pump. It is you pumping positive thoughts in your tank. The best fuel to have more energy is to avoid negative people."**
*--Rick Macci*

One of the most critical changes a billion dollar mind individual can make is surrounding themselves with the right people. Positive, enthusiastic, and motivating people encourage you to achieve your best and reach the highest level possible.

Watch what is said to you. If someone starts criticizing you, it can drag down your motivation and enthusiasm, leading to a negative cycle of self-defeating thoughts that can result in inefficiency, unproductive results, lack of motivation, and depression.

Immediately recognize negative individuals and distance- or even mentally detach from them. Become aware of their negative energy and reverse it with self-love immediately, keeping your mind healthy and productive.

As soon as your environment, thought patterns, and beliefs change your whole world changes, filling with ideas and effective actions to take you to the next level of your life.

If you are training with someone like Rick Macci or another professional and are high-achieving, you won't feel alone but inspired. It can be lonely when you are on the journey to success, striving for high performance and working harder than others.

The path of being ordinary, wasting time, enjoying lazing around, and eating unhealthfully is more easily done by followers, not leaders. Rick Macci is teaching even in the rainstorms, on a weekend, training students effortlessly, and with passion. Contrast this with 99% of other coaches who, whenever they even see a glimpse of rain, pick up their tennis balls and head home. A high-performing athlete doesn't feel encouraged if their coach heads home; they're the ones practicing in the rain. Good coaches and good associations are crucial to developing a successful mind.

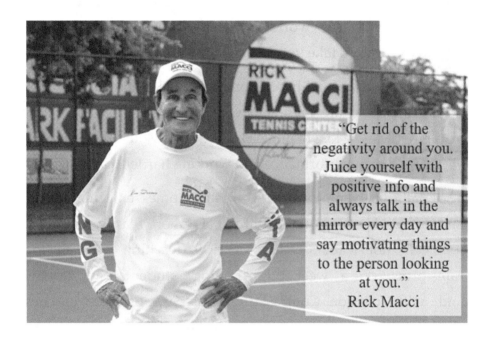

"Get rid of the negativity around you. Juice yourself with positive info and always talk in the mirror every day and say motivating things to the person looking at you."
Rick Macci

## Practical Exercise

Write down what is said to you in a journal every day, and if there are consistently negative people who infiltrate your mind, bombard you with negativity, even a mere 1% negative talk, make sure you are aware of it and distance yourself from those individuals.

_____

_____

_____

_____

_____

_____

_____

_____

_____

_____

_____

_____

_____

_____

# FIVE

# IMPROVE SENSORY INPUT THROUGH THE POWER OF VISUALIZATION

**"Practice in your mind first. See it, feel it, and then do it.
Dream it, feel it, smell it, touch it long before you even try it."**
*- Rick Macci*

Visualization is a crucial component of success. It strongly affects the sensory system as visualization alone can activate the brain's motor cortex. Visualization can stimulate the brain and even form more connections in the brain to help carry out a motor task. Visualizing your movement can help fire motor neurons even though the activity is not occurring, thus stimulating and strengthening motor neurons in those who are weak.

A 1950s experiment at the University of Chicago demonstrated how visualizing shooting free throws in basketball alone (without practice) improves free throw percentage.

Visualization is vital in all aspects, including significant events, speaking engagements, and all professional endeavors. Visualization helps clarify the actions and then associates the positive emotion of confidence to go along with it.

Adding visualization to practice can truly enhance your performance.

"Life is a reflection of what we visualize in our imagination."
Dr. Niva

**Practical Exercise**

Spend time every day visualizing tomorrow, how you will respond to specific, predictable patterns and how you will respond to unpredictable events. Think about it as if it's like a movie in your mind: smell it, feel it, enjoy it, hear it, and taste it. Write down, draw, and visualize your goals for the following month, in five years, and in ten years.

_____

_____

_____

_____

_____

_____

_____

_____

_____

_____

_____

_____

_____

_____

# SIX

# IMPROVE SENSORY INPUT THROUGH SELF-AWARENESS AND SELF-LOVE

"The best advice you will ever hear is when you
say positive things to yourself and listen."
*- Rick Macci*

Self-love is appreciating and valuing yourself. This is essential to mental strength as it involves maintaining a positive self-image, even in a negative environment or situation.

Practicing self-love involves following your passion by recognizing your inner self. That inner self may enjoy exercise, dance, yoga, eating certain types of food or clothes, or even specific types of people. Realizing, loving, and respecting that inner self is the true path to mental strength. Being honest and finding yourself is the first step to winning in life as it allows you to connect with your true self, find your goals, and strengthen your mind. Once you figure out what you truly desire and who you truly are, you don't need to have others to make decisions for you.

For example, Rick Macci, has not traveled much with his professional tennis players because he knows himself and enjoys training the students at his academy rather than traveling.

Essential steps to self-love include the acceptance of not being perfect. Another step is to stop comparing yourself to others or mentally putting yourself down. It is easy to fall into self-defeating traps by creating negativity with social media.

"Think of at least 10 things that you love about yourself and fill your heart with joy."
Dr. Niva

## Practical Exercise

Write down 10 things that you love about yourself. Commit today to refrain from comparing yourself or putting yourself down on social media. When this behavior recurs, stop engaging on social media and remind yourself of the things you love about yourself. Do the things you enjoy.

_____

_____

_____

_____

_____

_____

_____

_____

_____

_____

_____

_____

_____

_____

# SEVEN

# IMPROVE SENSORY INPUT THROUGH POSITIVE THOUGHTS

"Every day you feed your face with food.
Feed your brain with positive words and
the food will taste even better!"
*- Rick Macci*

Thoughts are the fundamentals for your success. Without successful thoughts, there is difficulty in achieving anything. We must have thoughts that make us happy, positive, confident, and successful. When our thoughts deviate from that path, it's time to reconnect with our true selves, find the strong *why* that motivates us to take difficult journeys and focus on things that make us happy. These things vary and differ for everyone, but they are important to recognize.

Watch the triggers that create in you a negative or depressed state. If you find yourself saying negative things, dragging in activity, or feeling unmotivated, think of this from a hunger, fatigue, lack of exercise, or lack of balance point of view.

Whatever is personal to you. Although these thoughts are inconsistent, they must be weeded out of our brain, actively and consistently.

Understand that failure is part of every journey, and the key to opening a new door to better opportunities awaits. Failure is an opportunity to learn and improve. Right or wrong is determined by our own thoughts.

"Every action and emotion in life is started by a thought. Take care of your thoughts as you would take care of a garden to create the life you desire."
Dr. Niva

**Practical Exercise**

Consistently watch what thoughts you generate and whether they are negative or positive. Write them down and figure out why you think a certain thought every hour or daily as needed. If the thoughts are negative, continue to weed them out as soon as they begin; these thoughts are not real. When you find patterns in how you think, you can analyze your flaws and predict your future reactions to a problem.

Consistently practice deleting thought patterns that are not useful, including ones of doubt, anxiety, fear, and any negativity holding you back from your next level of success.

If you have a water bottle (or anything you drink from consistently), place positive statements on it and say them to yourself as you drink it, feeding your mind with positive thoughts.

Tree bathing is a practice that involves cleansing your mind, and producing positive thoughts while deleting self generated negative thoughts, doubts, fears, worries, anxiety, or grudges while being amongst trees.

# EIGHT

# LETTING GO OF PAST MEMORIES

"The most important thing in life is next.
When you live in the past, you get passed."

*- Rick Macci*

One aspect of mind control is controlling our memories of the past. These memories have been deep-rooted since childhood and continue to maintain our actions as we grow older. We don't realize they are deeply rooted.

Think of childhood memories that were terrifying, scary, or even just memorable. The ones that instilled fear could be restricting you from moving on and succeeding. For example, a threatening experience with a neighbor and seeing a gun at a young age could translate into fear of others as an adult. Another experience could be a painful loss of a loved one associated with a condition like cancer, causing you to run away when you hear the word cancer. Recognizing this deep-rooted memory is crucial; letting go of it helps you heal and move on. These deep-rooted memories are extremely personal and can cause performance-related issues if they are not addressed.

The best athletes, performers, and highest achievers have learned how to let go of past mistakes quickly.

In fact, the best tennis players will forget the previous mistake or double fault immediately so they can focus on the next point.

The ability to forget the past is one of the most important mental strengthening exercises as it stops your mind from being paralyzed by the past and it allows you the freedom to focus on making the next moment as amazing as possible.

"Letting go of the thought patterns that do not help you can change your world!" Dr. Niva

## Practical Exercise

Practice thinking of the 10 most memorable moments of your childhood. Think about them, write them down, and then recognize how they influence your current life and thought patterns. If they have had negative influences, actively practice letting them go.

Take a memory from your past that could be painful and then switch it with a more pleasant memory the way you wanted it to go as soon as the painful memory appears in your mind.

_____

_____

_____

_____

_____

_____

_____

_____

_____

_____

_____

_____

# NINE

# FLIP COMPLICATED SENSORY INPUT SITUATIONS

"Make adversity your best friend. Having the
ability to flip it in your mind and turn Mr. Negative
into Mr. Positive is the key to unlocking any
door to find your true potential."

*- Rick Macci*

Many times, we can control simple sensory inputs. If there is a negative trigger, we can avoid it. We can choose to fill our minds with positive affirmations, positive associations, and visualizations. But there are times when the entire world can feel as if it's falling apart. This would include unexpected tragedies, natural disasters, the death of a loved one, a terminal illness, or obstacles during a competition, such as unfair advantages, illness, injuries, and unexpected environmental circumstances, to name a few.

During tough times, it is important to "flip it," as Rick Macci describes. Take a negative event and generate positive mental energy around it to turn the negative event into a positive winning force. For example, when Michael Jordan was booed in a crowd, he would flip the situation to propel him toward the win. He would play better. It's a natural tendency in champions to flip it; the alternative is to drown in negativity and inevitable loss. Champions in any area of life are no different than the next person, except for their ability to flip it. This is how they create ta billion dollar mind.

"Flipping it" involves reinterpreting a negative story into a positive one. Instead of telling yourself that you lost a match and are a no-good tennis player, try saying, "This loss is an opportunity for me to win next time, to improve and better myself." Reinterpreting events or flipping them can help make winning the desired outcome in every situation you encounter.

For example, when the great tennis player Roger Federer was playing in the wind, he said, "Playing in the wind was a blast." As Rick Macci says, always consider problems a mandatory part of the journey to the next issue. Bad situations can become good situations today if you flip the script and take a negative and turn it into a positive starting right now. For example, if you think it is cold, it just got colder.

Flipping a situation ultimately means that you will never lose due to a negative event.

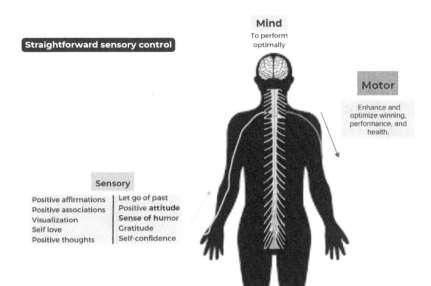

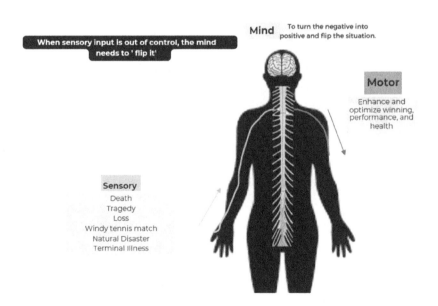

**Practical Exercise**

Every night, write down an adverse event or negative thought in your mind and practice flipping it or reinterpreting it to create a positive interpretation or outcome.

Minimize stressful situations by asking yourself, "Will this be significant in 10 years?" This allows you to see each circumstance from a different angle.

_____

_____

_____

_____

_____

_____

_____

_____

_____

_____

_____

_____

_____

_____

# TEN

# HUMOR TO IMPROVE MENTAL HEALTH AND RELAXATION

**"Laughter, fun, and joy help the body relax. Having the ability to look at things in the exact opposite light of the way we're expected to look at it can mean the difference between extraordinary and ordinary."**
*- Rick Macci*

You have likely heard the saying laughter is the best medicine. It's true. Laughing and humor can decrease mental stress. In addition, it has many other health benefits, such as increasing oxygen intake, reducing the stress response, relaxing muscles, improving the immune system, relieving pain, and improving your mood.

Laughter is comparable to aerobic exercise. Immediately after laughter there is a muscle relaxation response, which can last up to 45 minutes.

Humor can increase productivity, creative thinking, and trust. It helps with seeing things in a bigger perspective and taking things lightly. Incorporating it in your sensory toolbox is vital to improve your mental strength.

Fun and smiling trigger feelings of calm and intensity, creating the ideal mental and physical performance state. For example, tennis coach Rick Macci promotes a fun environment for students at his academy.

"You only live once,
but in tennis you get
to serve twice."
Dr. Niva

**Practical Exercise**

Find time to laugh every day.

Recognize what makes you laugh and keep that around you when stressed.

Practice smiling, especially when you feel pressure.

Do 10 things that are approved by the billion dollar-mind-you that create fun, laughter, and happiness. Practice those 10 things when swerving from a negative mindset to recalibrating yourself. Even if small or perceived as insignificant, sticking to what makes you happy is your first step toward positivity and happiness.

---

---

---

---

---

---

---

---

---

---

# ELEVEN

# POSITIVE ATTITUDE

"The greatest ever in anything had the most positive
attitude about everything. A positive attitude is
available on your calendar 24/7, and you have an open
invite. A bulletproof positive attitude and mindset is the
cornerstone of handling the zigs and zags, and the good,
the bad, and the ugly of every situation with which you
deal. Winners find a way and losers make excuses."
- *Rick Macci*

**A positive attitude requires zero percent talent.** Attitude is how
you respond to a certain event; having a positive attitude is the
key to being mentally tough.

When you find a positive in every action, you are on track to
look at the world through a different lens. A positive attitude
allows you to give 100%, and that is where you must start with
any practice. A positive attitude enables you to expect to win
rather than hoping to win.

Recognize that you are responsible for your thoughts and emotions. If you can switch from a negative to a positive attitude, it is 100% in your favor.

A positive attitude focuses on the positive of any situation or obstacle and expects positive results.

"For breakfast each morning
have an 8 ounce glass of
POSITIVITEA."
Rick Macci

**Practical Exercise**

Write in your journal how you can use a positive attitude to improve your situation. If, for example, there is an obstacle in life, list the ways a positive attitude alone could help overcome it or see it differently. Consider the below examples.

Create a good time even when you are losing.

Smile during a difficult time.

Have a positive future vision.

Maintain your thoughts, body posture, and outlook in an upbeat positive way consistently.

Respond to criticism or feedback positively.

Evaluate your thoughts and delete all your excuses, replacing them with positive solutions.

_____

_____

_____

_____

_____

_____

_____

_____

# TWELVE

# GRATITUDE

**"Gratitude is the number one energy drink
everybody should have daily."**
*- Rick Macci*

Gratitude is being thankful and appreciative; it comes from the latin work *gratia*, which means gratefulness. Gratitude is an appreciation of what is received and helps you acknowledge the goodness in your life. Gratitude improves positivity and helps you with health, relationships, and happiness.

Gratitude helps us feel more positive emotions, relish good experiences, improve our health, deal with adversity, and build strong relationships.

A study was done by two psychologists, Dr. Robert Emmons and Dr. Michael E. McCullogh, in which three groups wrote a few sentences each week: one expressing gratitude, another expressing criticism, and the third expressing neutrality. After 10 weeks, the gratitude writers were healthier and more optimistic.

Rick Macci remembers vividly how Venus, Serena, and Richard Williams would say thank you to him every day, and practiced their gratitude. This is an essential technique for your mental strength and life success.

**Practical Exercise**

Make it a daily activity to practice gratitude.

Every evening before you go to bed, list all the things you are grateful for, even if it's as simple as expressing thankfulness for your breath in a gratitude journal.

If there is someone you are grateful to, or for, say thank you to them before you go to bed in your mind. You might also write them a note in an email or text message as appropriate.

_____

_____

_____

_____

_____

_____

_____

_____

_____

_____

_____

_____

# THIRTEEN
# SELF-CONFIDENCE

**"Confidence is magnetic and the most important thing you can teach a child. When you expect yourself to do more and force yourself to do more, you will not have to anymore."**
*- Rick Macci*

Self-confidence is the ability to trust and believe in yourself to accomplish a task regardless of the obstacles. Be unapologetically bold with the decisions you make.

Self-confidence might be compared to the running water in a house. It keeps the house going when it's there, but has substantial negative consequences when it's not available. Confidence is the same—when it's lacking, it has significant, negative impact.

Having confidence is another crucial ingredient to a mentally strong diet; it is how you perceive achieving your goals. Confidence is important to mental strength and helps you take a risk, try new things, and get out of your comfort zone. Confidence allows you to take risks that give you the chance to be number one. Confident decisions are often the right decisions compared to those lacking confidence.

**Obtain confidence through repeated efforts of repetition, persistence, and practice. This results in reaching your goals without giving up.**

**Practical exercise**

Every morning, look in the mirror and tell yourself, "I believe in you."

Write down your achievements before you go to bed.

Stop comparing yourself to others and focus on improving yourself even if it means putting away social media to build confidence.

Surround yourself with people that believe in you.

Follow through on the promises you make yourself.

Set a goal and achieve it.

Recognize that your goal is to focus on your strengths, not to be perfect.

Delete your self-doubt immediately

Repetition, repetition, repetition in practice to perfect your thinking.

Do not give up—find pathways to obtain your goal.

Reject negative self-talk to boost your confidence.

Take feedback positively; consider it a contribution to your growth.

Be the ideal version of yourself.

Write a letter to yourself about the great things you have achieved.

"Never let your own self doubt stop you from living your dreams."
Dr. Niva

# CONCLUSION

"The most important thing you do is right now. Think like that and your focus and energy will grow every day. Changing your mind is much better than changing the channel. The difference between great and good is the microscopic, invisible, inner, intangible of the mind."

*- Rick Macci*

The mind is a weapon we can use for or against us. As we conclude this book, the mind is a game where we play against our true selves. The concept of this book is to help you win the game against yourself and conquer your mind. At first, you must take a journey through your own mind and understand the mental programming. After this understanding, you are then able to win, you versus your mind.

If you control your sensory input and feed your mind consistently with positive, happy, successful thoughts, you can obtain your desired results. You can form a mental bubble of sorts that allows you to have an iron, billion-dollar mind.

Positive affirmations
Positive associations
Visualization
Self love
Positive thoughts
Let go of past
Positive attitude
Sense of humor
Gratitude
Self-confidence

Mental
bubble

Mind
becomes a
POSITIVITY
GENERATOR
allowing for
ultimate
focus and
belief to
achieve goals

"Mental Power starts with having power over oneself."
Dr. Niva

**Is your mind in your control? Test yourself below with the following mental challenges to find out!**

#1 Eat less than being 100% full.
Date accomplished:

#2 Take a tiny bite of dessert and save rest for later or do not eat the dessert at all.
Date accomplished:

#3 Eat something that you don't like but is nutritious for you.
Date accomplished:

#4 Do one extra repetition of an exercise when you are at the gym and finished.
Date accomplished:

#5 Do something you are afraid of.
Date accomplished:

#6 Do something you have self-doubt about.
Date accomplished:

#7 Think a positive thought about something or someone you dislike.
Date accomplished:

#8 Take a deep breathe when angry and do not lose your anger.
Date accomplished:

#9 Learn something new daily.
Date accomplished:

#10 Stretch or do a few exercises while waiting in a long line.
Date accomplished:

# Test your mental strength with these challenges (continued)

#11 Practice with loud distractions, unfair conditions, and a cheater.
Date accomplished:

#12 Smile and do not react when you feel insulted.
Date accomplished:

#13 Forgive yourself of a mistake.
Date accomplished:

#14 Listen to understand the full story before you react.
Date accomplished:

#15 Do not judge someone by their cover.
Date accomplished:

#16 Do not take no for an answer.
Date accomplished:

#17 Love to be competitive no matter what.
Date accomplished:

#18 Take criticism with joy so you can improve.
Date accomplished:

#19 Take a risk that will help your reach your goal.
Date accomplished:

#20 Recognize a limiting thought, delete it, and replace it with an empowering one.
Date accomplished:

#21 Take ownership of your life. Prepare your clothes, bags, or goals for the next day the night before.
Date accomplished:

# ABOUT THE AUTHORS

In 1991, the world famous, legendary, and immortalized tennis coach Rick Macci was about to change the face of tennis forever. That year, he took his biggest career risk: visiting two then-unknown sisters, Venus and Serena Williams, in Compton, California. He saw breathtaking potential in the sisters, but taking them on as his students would be risky.

Yet Rick Macci's unwavering belief in Venus and Serena, along with their own belief and dedication, skillfully nurtured by Rick, created the two most successful female athletes the world of tennis has ever seen. The magic ingredient was Rick's unshakeable belief in himself and his newly discovered phenoms. It's that magic that he's shared with all of his present and past students, including Jennifer Capriati, Andy Roddick, Maria Sharapova, Sofya Bielinska,"Elizabeth (Elli) Mandlik, Sofia Kenin, Tommy Ho, Anastasia Myskina, Mary Pierce, Vince Spadea, Bethanie

Mattek, Vicki Duvall, Christian Ruud, Karim Alami, Tina Pisnik, Ulises Blanch, Darwin Blanch, Dali Blanch, Stefan Kozlov and hundreds of Hollywood celebrities and world dignitaries. They've all had their lives and careers changed by Macci's magic.

*"Rewiring a player's mindset to look at their playing style and life through a different lens is the key to connecting their mental fitness to physical game-readiness."* – Rick Macci

Rick Macci is the USA's premier advocate for the game of tennis and the #1 tennis coach in the world of the past century, leading by example with all of his students. His truest gift is in his corrective techniques and uncanny ability to nimbly adjust flaws, attitudes, and habits, not only in his student's game but in their thinking. Moving the mindset of an aspiring champion higher into an exceptionally positive state requires focus from both the coach and the student. Accomplishing this consistently is something that, throughout his career and life, has given Rick a magical edge in his role as a tennis and life coach. Experts agree that Rick's insight into explaining and presenting psychological triggers that critically influence an athlete's performance is a gift few coaches possess or deliver.

Achieving global respect from his industry and the public is an unmatched source of pride and gratitude for Macci. Tallying the scores of **40 years** of motivating proteges, their families, friends, Hollywood celebrities, and dignitaries have produced legendary results.

His accomplishments include not only a **7-time USPTA Coach of The Year award** and the **youngest person ever inducted into the USPTA Hall of Fame**, but also his students who have achieved the following:

5 ranked #1 in the world
8 Olympic gold medals
12 ranked top 10 in the world
52 grand slam singles titles
86 grand slam singles titles in singles, doubles, mixed
328 USTA Jr National Titles since 1985

Rick's regimen is just as legendary as his teaching. Waking daily at 3:00 a.m., he sets a standard of excellence that motivates everyone, including his highest-performing students. His book Macci Magic details some of his processes, and he also hosts the podcast "Game Set Life" with David Meltzer, impacting thousands of players with his positivity, work ethic, and honest approach to life and tennis. He has been immortalized in the movie King Richard for his instrumental role in the early development of Venus and Serena Williams' incredible tennis careers.

These days, Rick, who hails originally from Greenville, Ohio, still works his magic from the tennis court to Wall Street as an in-demand guest speaker, both in-person and virtual. He lights up any interview. His relatable storytelling about the game of tennis and life is epic. He uses that edge to teach other coaches how to motivate and communicate with their students to "deliver the goods."

Rick has appeared on "60 Minutes," the "Today Show," "Good Morning America," "Inside Edition," "Day One," and many programs across CBS, NBC, ABC, CNN, USA, ESPN, the Tennis Channel, BBC, Fox news, Fox business, hundreds of podcasts, and sports-talk radio shows worldwide.

Connect with Rick Macci on his website at RickMacci.com.

**Dr. Nivedita (Niva) Uberoi Jerath** is from Augusta, Georgia and found herself blessed to have trained at some of the best institutions in the country– Harvard University (for under-graduate and for neurology residency), Mayo Clinic College of Medicine, and University of Iowa for her neuromuscular and clinical neurophysiology fellowships. At the University of Iowa, she received a Muscular Dystrophy Association Grant to study driving ability in patients with CMT1A. Passionate to help her patients, she was honored to be a Director of Neuromuscular Medicine in Orlando where since 2019, she has led her program to be recognized nationally by the Muscular Dystrophy Association, ALS association, Hereditary Neuropathy Foundation, American Association of Electrodiagnostic Medicine, and the Myasthenia Gravis Foundation of America. She is also the principal investigator for multiple neuromuscular clinical trials. She specializes in connecting with her patients and in solving some of the most challenging neuromuscular cases. She wants not only to be an icon for modern neuromuscular medicine but also to celebrate her patients with neuromuscular disorders and to recognize their amazing achievements despite their disabilities that were most often no fault of their own.

She has written numerous papers and books and enjoys making a difference in her patients' lives. This particular topic is one of her passions, as she was undefeated in tennis while playing in the Southern Tennis Association for many years. She used mental strength to be a junior tennis champion and get through the long years of medical school, training in some of the most prestigious universities including Harvard for undergraduate and residency, Mayo Clinic for medical school and University of Iowa for her fellowship and masters. While she treats patients who are physically weak and paralyzed, she has recognized a strong need to help many all over the world who are mentally weak and as a result mentally paralyzed. She is passionate to help heal those who are mentally paralyzed to help them reach their full potential.

In her youth, Rick Macci recruited her to his academy after she beat one of his students in a tournament. She is blessed to have trained in tennis with him and describes him as "aMACCIng". Rick never made her feel alone on her path to achieving her highest potential, reaching for the top, or making successful choices, such as going to Harvard University rather than being a professional athlete. A strong billion-dollar mind that allows for making intelligent successful choices is crucial to reaching one's dreams in life.

Follow Dr. Niva on Facebook, LinkedIn, YouTube, Instagram (doctor.niva) or https://drniva.com

**Photography Credits**

Jeny Roc (pages 7, 17, 27, 37)

Kimberly Jefcoat (page 17)

Ziva Aum Reddy (page 32)

Kenneth Appelbaum (pages 22, 52, 70, 73, 76)

**Cover Credit:** Kamir Kamaldeen Tope

**Book Editing:** Bonni Rogers, Green Lady Publishing

73646590R00049